THE
COMPASSIONATE LEADER:
NAVIGATING SELFLESSNESS IN LEADERSHIP

A guide to leadership that emphasizes selflessness and the principles of selfless leadership.

DR. TYRONE SPEARS

BOOK SHORT DESCRIPTION

In "The Compassionate Leader: Navigating Selflessness in Leadership," [Dr. Tyrone Spears] explores a fresh approach to leadership that goes beyond traditional paradigms. The book demonstrates how selflessness can be a powerful force for inspiring teams, building trust, and fostering collaboration. Discover the transformative impact of leading with empathy, humility, and a genuine commitment to the well-being of others. This guide is essential for leaders who seek to make a lasting impact in today's dynamic business environment.

TABLE OF CONTENTS

Book Short Description ---------------------------------- ii

INTRODUCTION ------------------------------------- **V**

CHAPTER ONE ---------------------------------------**1**
Understanding the Qualities of a
Selfless Leader -- 1

CHAPTER TWO --------------------------------------**5**
Ten Key Principles of Selfless Leadership---------------- 5

CHAPTER THREE ---------------------------------- **13**
Examining Selflessness within the Principles of Servant
Leadership -- 13

CHAPTER FOUR ----------------------------------- **17**
The Impact of Selflessness on the Effectiveness of Servant Leadership -- 17

CHAPTER FIVE ------------------------------------- **21**
Exploring Effective Selfless Leadership: A Comprehensive Look -- 21

CHAPTER SIX -------------------------------------- **25**
The Mastery of Decision-Making ---------------------- 25

CHAPTER SEVEN — **29**
Advantages of Embracing Selflessness in Leadership — 29

CHAPTER EIGHT — **33**
Leadership and the Importance of Self-Awareness — 33

CHAPTER NINE — **37**
Navigating Difficulties and Seizing Opportunities in a Selfless Leadership Framework — 37

CHAPTER TEN — **47**
Characteristics of Successful and Unsuccessful Leadership — 47

CHAPTER ELEVEN — **57**
Examinations of Leaders Demonstrating Selflessness — 57

CHAPTER TWELVE — **63**
Developing Fostering Selfless Leadership through the Principles of Servant Leadership — 63

CHAPTER THIRTEEN — **73**
Profiles of Leadership — 73

CHAPTER FOURTEEN — **77**
Closing Thoughts on The Selfless Leader — 77

Introduction

This book aims to explore the core principles of selflessness in leadership, examining the principles of selfless leadership as a guiding framework. Through an in-depth examination of its characteristics, strategies for growth, challenging circumstances, and its influence on businesses and society, our goal is to provide a valuable resource for individuals seeking to develop their leadership skills. We aim to inspire a mindset that values professional growth over personal gain, fostering a ripple effect of positive change and ethical leadership in our ever-changing world.

Chapter One

Understanding the Qualities of a Selfless Leader

An approach to management called "selfless leadership" prioritizes the growth and well-being of the team over the goals of the organization or the leader. Unlike a typical leader, a selfless leader prioritizes personal growth and mentorship over solely accomplishing organizational goals. It begins with a deep-rooted commitment to prioritize the needs of others more than anything else.

Here are the steps to cultivate the qualities of a selfless leader:

Be a Role Model.

Being a leadership guide means consistently setting an example for your team. Being a selfless leader requires the ability to adapt to any challenge that your team may face. Your team may feel more motivated to actively participate in their work and contribute to the assignment when they observe your willingness to put in the same amount of effort and discipline as they do.

Show people the Significance of their Roles.

When employees understand the significance of their contributions to the organization's success, they tend to feel more empowered and motivated to put in extra effort. It is important to ensure that your team members understand the significance of their work and how it contributes to the overall success of the company.

Promote a Culture of Teamwork and active Participation from Employees.

Selfless leaders excel at ensuring their teams feel valued and respected, with a strong emphasis on fostering open communication and active participation. When you proactively foster collaboration within your team and actively seek their input on how to enhance the organization, it demonstrates your genuine concern for their opinions and value for their efforts. This can inspire your team to give their utmost effort to produce work of higher quality.

Empower your team to reach their full Potential.

Leaders who genuinely care about the growth and

development of their team members prioritize their own leadership skills and actively support their team members in becoming exceptional leaders. Encouraging your team to actively participate in ongoing education and employee development programs can greatly enhance their knowledge and skills.

Encouraging team members to take active leadership roles during group projects can be quite beneficial. When individuals perceive your dedication to their professional development, they become more receptive to suggestions aimed at enhancing their work.

Take the time to Personally care for your team Members.

To become an effective leader, it is crucial to genuinely care about your team members on a personal level. Offering empathy and advice can contribute to a more positive work-life balance for your employees and enhance their ability to manage personal stress. When your team recognizes the value of their individual contributions and feels appreciated, their motivation and job satisfaction increase, leading to higher-quality work and a more positive work environment.

Seeking Input from Others

In order to continuously enhance their leadership skills and make a positive impact on their team, selfless leaders should always be on the lookout for opportunities for growth. Motivate your team members to share their ideas for enhancing workflow and contributing to the company's success. Encourage your team members to feel empowered to approach you with suggestions and consistently seek feedback from those who need to provide it.

Chapter Two

Ten Key Principles of Selfless Leadership

So, what exactly does it mean to become a selfless leader? There are several key qualities that are commonly found in selfless leaders. Follow these ten guidelines to effectively apply selfless leadership to your team.

1. Pay attention and be attentive.

Listening is essential for effective selfless leadership. Give your undivided attention to team members when they are speaking. Please refrain from any interruptions. It is a simple method to ensure your team feels appreciated and understands your concern. Successful leaders understand the importance of actively engaging with their team and valuing their input. They provide many opportunities for all members to express their thoughts and actively listen to both spoken and unspoken messages.

2. Understanding and compassion

Understanding the various facets of empathy and selfless leadership essentially involves developing a deep understanding of your team. Explore what drives them and gain an understanding of their strengths and weaknesses. By following this approach, you can empower your team members to showcase their strengths and support them in addressing any weaknesses they may have.

Effective selfless leaders demonstrate genuine care for their team members. They recognize the importance of their team members' personal well-being and how it positively impacts their professional performance.

They appreciate the viewpoints of others and approach situations with a receptive mindset. As a leadership guide, it is crucial for selfless leaders to prioritize showing their team members that they genuinely care about them and are willing to assist with personal matters whenever possible.

3. Recovery

You have the privilege of supporting team members who have experienced challenging work environments in the past.

Successful leaders understand the importance of addressing and resolving issues before embarking on new goals and ventures.

For instance, your team might have faced a setback last quarter because of a disagreement among team members. In order to tackle the upcoming challenges of this quarter, it is crucial for the team to prioritize healing and reach a consensus. Effective leaders ensure that their team is equipped with the necessary knowledge, support, and resources to perform their jobs successfully.

Rest assured: The journey towards healing is not as daunting as it may appear. It entails fostering a harmonious work environment that places a high value on achieving a healthy work-life balance. It is also about providing individuals with the tools they need to succeed so that they feel like a valued member of the team.

Developing self-awareness is crucial for personal growth and success.

Successful leaders have a deep understanding of themselves and their teams. Self-recognition involves the capacity to reflect, explore one's emotions and actions, and consider their influence on the people around them. Understanding your team's strengths and weaknesses is crucial. However, it is equally crucial to take some time for self-reflection. Assess your strengths and weaknesses and determine how you can contribute to the overall team. Then, utilize yourself in ways that benefit the team and organization. Understanding your own limitations can provide valuable insights into how to effectively utilize your team's strengths.

4. Convincing others

Efficient income processes may also come to mind when considering persuasion. However, we are discussing a different topic now. Effective leaders inspire and persuade team members. While a traditional leader may dictate tasks to team members, a selfless leader explains the rationale behind a particular approach or method. Effective leaders use persuasive techniques to build consensus and gain support from their entire team. By doing so, they make sure that every team member is emotionally committed to the team's overall success.

5. Conceptualization

Effective leaders understand the importance of looking beyond small tasks and communicating the larger goals to their teams. They assist their team in understanding their roles and staying motivated, all while keeping the employer's long-term objectives and goals in mind.

It is important for you to have a clear understanding of your role as a leader and as someone who employs others. Because, without guidance, how else will you navigate and succeed in leading your team?

6. Looking ahead

Effective leaders understand the value of learning from both failures and successes, using past experiences to make informed decisions. They develop a keen awareness of the current situation, understand the impact of their choices, and then guide their team to do the same.

Applying the knowledge gained from past experiences is crucial in selfless leadership, as it allows you and your team to constantly evolve and thrive.

Project post-mortems, or retrospectives, are an invaluable tool for evaluating successes and areas for improvement, allowing you to fine-tune your approach with each new project.

7. Embracing the principles of stewardship

Stewardship is all about setting a positive example for others to follow. As a leader, it is essential to establish the tone for your team by leading by example and not expecting others to do tasks you wouldn't do yourself. Successful selfless leaders are highly respected and understand the significance of their duties. They confidently uphold and protect the acceptance given to them in their role and effectively communicate this to their team.

One way I implemented this was by being the first person to sign up for the 2:00 a.m. slot. If something goes wrong, I will handle the situation with composure and grace.

8. Dedication to the development of individuals

Selfless leaders have a remarkable ability to inspire their teams to achieve personal growth. They exemplify their dedication to the professional growth of their team members by leading by example and providing numerous opportunities for advancement. They also take the time to understand their employees' personal goals and provide them with projects or additional responsibilities to support their growth.

We provide an annual conference price range to help team contributors develop the skills they need to excel in their roles. As a leader your perspective is limited. Having a comprehensive view of performance, including feedback from peers and direct reports, allows you to gain a holistic understanding and uncover valuable opportunities for growth.

9. Creating a sense of community

Successful leaders inspire teamwork and active participation within their organizations. They highly appreciate the feedback from every individual on their team and encourage them to openly share their thoughts and actively participate in group discussions.

They offer various avenues for interaction through social activities, workspace layout, or even informal meetings with conversations unrelated to work.

10. Discovering the intersection of selflessness and servant leadership

The intersection of selflessness and servant management brings together essential concepts that deeply influence how leaders engage, motivate, and support their followers.

Servant management, at its core, revolves around leaders prioritizing the needs of others over their own. It embodies a mindset where leaders prioritize serving others, wholeheartedly committing themselves to the growth, development, and welfare of their groups or communities. This approach emphasizes empathy, humility, and an authentic dedication to serving others.

Selflessness, when it comes to leadership, embodies a similar ethos. It entails a willingness to set apart private hobbies, egos, and objectives for the extra top of these being led. Selfless leaders' function comes from a viewpoint in which their primary goal is to support, uplift, and empower others, even supposing it approaches non-public sacrifice.

The intersection between those two ideas is where management transcends mere authority and management. It is a space where leaders harness the electricity of empathy and humility to create environments of belief, collaboration, and boom. Here, leaders do not try to find reputation or glory; as an alternative, they derive fulfillment from being in their groups or as followers.

This intersection manifests as leaders who actively concentrate, empathize, and apprehend the needs of their fans. They prioritize mentorship, guidance, and improvement, developing avenues for individuals to flourish. These leaders show off authenticity, integrity, and transparency in their moves, fostering a lifestyle of agreeing with and recognizing.

Moreover, the intersection of selflessness and servant management encourages a shift in awareness from personal achievements to collective success. It promotes a feeling of shared purpose and a dedication to the greater good, aligning the aspirations of both leaders and fans closer to a common imaginative and prescient.

Chapter Three

Examining Selflessness within the Principles of Servant Leadership

Analyzing selflessness within the standards of servant leadership entails a deeper exploration beyond the list of points. It is information on how each principle embodies and reinforces the concept of selflessness.

This notion of carrying forms the muse upon which selflessness is built within this management framework.

Selfless leaders display empathy by actively listening to and understanding others' views and wishes. By empathizing, they placed themselves in others' footwear, demonstrating a selfless act of, in reality, caring about the experiences and feelings of their fans.

Selflessness is obvious in a selfless leader's inclination toward restoration and compassion. They devote themselves to aiding others in their non-public and professional improvement, focusing on the well-being of their crew members beyond mere professional success.

A selfless chief operates with an eager cognizance of the effect of their selections on others. They use persuasion in preference to coercion, aligning others' pursuits with organizational desires and demonstrating a commitment to serving collective wishes rather than non-public agendas.

Servant leaders have an extended period and a selfless attitude. They conceptualize techniques that benefit the more excellent, thinking about the well-being and boom of their fans and the network they serve.

Selflessness is embedded in a servant leader's dedication to stewardship. They take responsibility for nurturing the capability and boom of their followers, viewing leadership as a selfless obligation to serve and empower others.

A selfless leader's recognition of constructing a community inside their organization. They foster an environment of acceptance as true with collaboration and mutual admiration, wherein selflessness is exemplified via the emphasis on teamwork and collective achievement.

Selflessness within selfless leadership ideas is not only a single function but an interwoven material that runs through each principle. It is a dedication to putting others' needs first, empathizing with their experiences, and actively working in the direction of their growth and well-being. These standards collectively form a frontrunner who embodies selflessness, growing a fine and impactful management style that inspires and uplifts others.

Chapter Four

The Impact of Selflessness on the Effectiveness of Servant Leadership

Selflessness acts as the cornerstone of servant leadership, amplifying its effectiveness in several ways. When a leader embodies selflessness:

Fosters Trust and Empathy

Selflessness cultivates an environment of agreement and empathy. Leaders who prioritize others' desires create a feeling of mental safety, encouraging open communication and collaboration.

Inspires loyalty and commitment.

By placing the well-being of their followers first, selfless leaders encourage loyalty and commitment. Individuals experience value, leading to increased dedication to collective goals, imagination, and vision.

Strengthens Relationships

Selflessness builds sturdy, meaningful relationships primarily based on mutual appreciation and expertise. Leaders who certainly care for their team foster a culture of guidance and harmony.

Encourages personal growth

A selfless leader nurtures non-public growth and development among their crew members. By investing in people's lives', we empowered them and stimulated them to excel.

Promotes collaboration and innovation.

A selfless chief encourages collaboration and innovation. When people experience their contributions being valued, they are willing to prioritize thoughts and desires together toward commonplace dreams.

Create a positive organizational culture

Selflessness contributes to a tremendous organizational tradition. When leaders prioritize the needs of their group, it sets a precedent for a way of life of care, aid, and shared values.

Increasing Organizational Resilience

Servant leaders' selflessness builds resilience within organizations. Teams led with the aid of selfless leaders are better prepared to address challenges, adapt to change, and preserve morale for the duration of tough instances.

Amplifies the Impact of Servant Leadership Principles.

Selflessness amplifies the effect of other servant leadership concepts. Empathy, listening, and stewardship are impactful while grounded in real care and difficulty for others.

Selflessness acts as a catalyst that magnifies the effectiveness of servant leadership. It forms the bedrock upon which belief, collaboration, private growth, and a fantastic organizational culture flourish, driving outstanding overall performance and the belief of shared desires. When leaders prioritize selflessness, they pave the way for transformative and sustainable leadership that empowers people and fosters collective fulfillment.

Chapter Five

Exploring Effective Selfless Leadership: A Comprehensive Look

The four attributes that are principal to the selfless management framework.

SERVICE TO OTHERS

Selfless leadership revolves around the fundamental choice to serve others. Leaders set apart their self-serving movements as an effective way to include the function of a selfless to both their team and the organization.

The philosophy is cemented with the aid of encouraging crew members to carry out their duties at their own pace. In their interactions with team members, selfless leaders emphasize and anticipate the function of a servant. Success is, therefore, inevitable, as the chief serves the team by spotting and encouraging the team's capabilities to achieve organizational dreams.

INTEGRATED WORK ETHIC

The connection among people, groups, and society is a crucial ethical element of portrayal. It emphasizes the significance of inspiring people to keep their integrity and ethical standards in all components of their lives, whether personal or professional.

Instilling an Experience of Community

Selfless management strives to build a sense of community among employees as a way to achieve organizational objectives. A network is a set of individuals with commonplace social, monetary, and political pursuits living in a single place or society.

POWER-SHARING IN SELECTION MAKING

By sharing the decision-making strength vested in them, selfless leaders demonstrate selfless leadership in others. The principle shows that the simplest technique to achieve organizational success is by delegating strength instead of preserving it to oneself. Power-sharing is achieved through encouraging worker talents and participation and creating an empowering environment within the corporation. The movements create a nicely inspired body of workers that drives employees to work towards accomplishing organizational goals.

The servant control philosophy is characterized by an inverted pyramid shape, with selfless leaders positioned at the bottom and employees and numerous stakeholders located at the pinnacle. This technique stands in stark contrast to the conventional hierarchical leadership style.

WHY IS LEADERSHIP IMPORTANT?

Anyone can be a leader. Everyone has leadership abilities within them; they are all simply at differing developmental stages. It takes time to exercise and toughen them; you need to put money into developing those skills and committing to growth. Becoming a selfless leader means putting the wishes of others before your own and continuously developing the ten characteristics listed above.

And do not forget that everybody learns at a one-of-a-kind pace. Keep gaining knowledge of, developing, and serving others. You can also look at several of the assets below to learn how you can become a selfless leader.

Leadership is important for the success of an organization because it provides guidance and purpose and helps others understand the long-term strategies and goals of a business. Here are reasons to value effective leadership:

VISION

Successful leadership creates a clear vision of what the organization can achieve. Leaders provide a roadmap outlining the steps and resources their company needs to arrive at its preferred destination.

COMMUNICATION

Leaders assist in explaining the vision and mission of the organization to employees. This provides direction and allows everybody to perceive the roles that suit their talents and reports. Through clear conversation, leaders inspire their subordinates to behave for the actualization of objectives.

Chapter Six

The Mastery of Decision-Making

Decision-making is one of the top leadership skills. Successful leadership makes the best decisions for the organization in all situations. Leaders are experts at making the right decisions based on the prevailing circumstances. They weigh their organization's strengths and weaknesses to ensure their choices put them at an advantage now and in the future.

PASSION

Leaders are passionate about their vision and infect others with their energy to achieve it. Effective leadership inspires others to buy into the company's objectives and provides a powerful reason for everyone to remain dedicated to their duties.

GUIDANCE

Once employees know what to do to deliver on projects, effective leaders oversee their work to ensure they perform their roles effectively. Leaders make sure employee efforts align with organizational goals for improved efficiency.

COMMITMENT

Effective leaders are dedicated to the fulfillment of their company and its personnel. They remain focused on the company's long-term goals and do not allow temporary setbacks to dampen their spirits. When they face a setback, good leaders motivate their teams and help them see beyond the problems preventing them from reaching the common goal.

INTEGRITY

Successful leadership teaches the organization ethical values. Regardless of their problems, successful leaders do the right things to achieve their goals. For them, integrity, truthfulness, and fairness are core attributes they want to see in their company and its relations with contractors and clients.

CONFIDENCE

Leaders help subordinates excel at their work and in every aspect of life by expressing confidence in their abilities. They listen to employees' worries about their work, provide positive feedback, and ensure the office environment brings out the best in them.

MORALE

Leadership boosts staff morale by winning their trust. It assures employees of the leader's confidence in their abilities to deliver on the vision and mission of the organization. High morale among employees reduces distraction and motivates them to devote their energies to achieving organizational goals.

GROWTH

The best leaders create an environment where others can grow. They are open to innovative ideas and methods of achieving results and are flexible enough to admit their mistakes. Successful leaders encourage subordinates to provide input on how to improve work processes and reward excellence to increase creativity and loyalty.

COORDINATION

Effective leadership balances personal interests with organizational objectives. Leaders know that employees have personal reasons for working with their company. They create an environment where the organization can achieve its goals without sacrificing employee satisfaction.

Chapter Seven

Advantages of Embracing Selflessness in Leadership

Stronger groups

By serving the group, selfless leaders collect the honor of their teammates, which increases collaboration, ends in efficient behavior, instills concord, and builds more potent teams.

A conducive running environment

Working alongside the leader in an employer's superb operating surroundings, wherein interactions are more positive and there is much less opposition to electrifying the chief via selfish political squabbles.

Alignment of private and professional goals

The aid and encouragement of private and professional improvement from a selfless leader permit personnel to align their private and professional objectives with organizational desires.

Alignment improves worker engagement, commitment, and loyalty to the company, ultimately increasing productivity and profit.

Improved organizational agility

Teams that receive help from their leaders are extra flexible in the face of changing surroundings, handing over an agile organization.

Professional improvement, supported with the aid of leaders, augments employee mastery and improvement processes in which strengths are more advantageous and weaknesses are addressed.

Leadership schooling

By running alongside their selfless leaders, team members discover ways to take responsibility and possession, accelerating their leadership skills.

Employee motivation

Selfless management improves employee motivation, which inspires the courage to be more innovative and revolutionary.

A people-oriented corporate way of life

The philosophy strengthens and develops a human-oriented corporate way of life.

Decreases worker turnover

Empowered individuals may be suggested to reside within the organization and preserve a more in-depth proximity to attaining the employer's objectives.

Chapter Eight

Leadership and the Importance of Self-Awareness

Self-awareness in leadership is the knowledge of how your personal development, behavior, and competencies influence your interactions with the people around you, specifically within the context of business. Self-conscious leaders actively replicate how others perceive their words and movements and work to exchange their processes on the way to lead their friends more efficiently. Self-attention ends in private manipulation and growth, which allow leaders to use their strengths in manual teams to achieve viable outcomes.

Why is self-awareness in leadership important?

Attaining self-awareness is important in leadership for many reasons, including the following:

ASSISTING LEADERS IN MAKING BETTER ALTERNATIVES: Effective leaders use self-focus to control their behavior and relationships. Leaders can expand their self-expertise to better catch up on their natural tendencies and competencies as they make choices in their place of work.

IMPACTING A COMPANY'S FINANCES: Companies may rely on self-aware leaders to be successful. Companies with greater success can also improve their financial standing.

Helping leaders understand what they bring to their role: Understanding their strengths in both industry knowledge and personal characteristics helps leaders perform their responsibilities within an organization better.

ALLOWING LEADERS TO BE PRACTICAL WITH THEIR EXPECTATIONS: Part of effective leadership is inspiring a team to paint in the direction of growth and meeting dreams. Self-conscious leaders recognize the way to balance what they want their crew to perform with the creative vision they carry to the institution.

Characteristics of Self-Awareness in Leadership

Here is a list of the characteristics of self-conscious leaders:

Reflective: A part of self-awareness comes from reflecting on your thoughts, phrases, and moves as you communicate with others.

OBSERVANT: Self-conscious leaders pay attention to what is taking place around them by following cues from their surroundings.

EMPATHETIC: Understanding the needs of others facilitates self-aware leaders' ability to relate to the ones they lead.

PERCEPTIVE: Anticipating the outcome of a situation is another important trait of self-aware leadership.

RESPONSIVE: Self-conscious leaders employ lively listening. They can adapt based totally on the reactions of others.

SELF-MANAGED: Self-conscious leaders can control their personal words and actions.

DISCERNING: Self-cognizance comes from making sensible selections about how you may cope with a situation.

ADAPTABLE: Self-aware leaders investigate a situation and reply by way of converting their behaviors.

Chapter Nine

Navigating Difficulties and Seizing Opportunities in a Selfless Leadership Framework

The theory needs to define the role of morality in selfless leadership clearly.

Selfless leaders also need to possess good enough expertise in their careers and the business as a whole.

Selfless leaders might also need greater motivation to serve, rendering the concept impractical.

Selfless management is predicated on the moral framework of its team.

The selfless management idea may be time-consuming for leaders, requiring greater effort, and that is a tough painting.

The authenticity wanted for selfless leadership is daunting and tough to reap.

Selfless leaders may be perceived as weak due to diminishing formal authority.

Employees are expected to make decisions and personalize them, a situation that could manifest when a worker reveals it is tough to see the larger picture and needs extra self-assurance to make choices that drive the commercial enterprise ahead.

Consultative decision-making can lead to slower selection-making.

HOW TO IMPROVE SELF-AWARENESS IN LEADERSHIP

Consider these strategies to help you improve your level of self-awareness in your leadership style:

KNOW YOURSELF

Since you are the only constant in changing workplace circumstances, it can be helpful to know your strengths and weaknesses. The ongoing manner of self-reflection powers self-cognizance. Emotional intelligence, that is, the potential to understand feelings in yourself and others, additionally impacts your recognition. Knowing yourself also means determining your internal standard of right and wrong. Your beliefs and behaviors help determine this standard.

IDENTIFY HOW OTHER PEOPLE REACT TO YOU.

One way you can assess how your actions affect others in the workplace is by observing or reflecting on how they react to you. Identify what factors cause them to respond in a certain way. This helps you understand your impact on others.

Gather feedback from trusted contacts.

While it can be challenging to separate your personal bias as you assess yourself, asking others to give input is one way to gain a broader picture of who you are and how you relate to others. Self-aware leaders may ask friends, family, and coworkers they trust to give insight about specific traits as they seek to better themselves.

FIND WAYS YOU CAN SHOW MORE EMPATHY.

Considering the feelings of others as you communicate and make decisions is another way to act self-aware as a leader. Paying attention to the emotional needs of those you lead can help guide your decisions and relationships as a self-aware leader. Be mindful of others' body language while you speak with them to gain insight into their emotions.

Be wise about your traits.

Be mindful of your circumstances so you know when to use a certain trait in each situation. Leverage your strengths to achieve positive results. Acting with self-awareness means evaluating whether you are making the right choices to meet your goals and advance the goals of others. You can also aim to build your emotional intelligence. Use online tools and books to learn how to be considerate of the emotions of your teammates. Learn how to maximize your introspection to understand yourself and those around you better.

Look for Patterns.

To achieve more self-awareness as a leader, determine what makes you the best you can be and strive toward those outcomes. Notice when you receive a positive response from your communication and actions as you interact with your team. Work to improve those traits and use them as much as possible.

PRACTICE SELF-EVALUATION

Those who are self-aware continually process and reflect on their situations. Practice this before, during, and after the conversation. Use your emotional intelligence and empathy to assess how you impact others through your characteristics.

SELFLESS LEADERSHIP vs. TRADITIONAL LEADERSHIP

Selfless leadership and traditional management utilize different techniques for leadership and bring extraordinary outcomes. Below are some of the principal variations between the two sorts of leadership philosophies.

COMPARISON WITH TRADITIONAL LEADERSHIP MODELS

Comparing selfless leadership with traditional management models presents treasured insights into their fundamental variations in approach, values, and consequences. Here is an exploration of the contrast:

Traditional leadership models

Hierarchy and Control: Traditional fashions often emphasize hierarchical systems in which electricity and manipulation are centralized at the top.

Focus on Results: Prioritizing consequences and productivity frequently takes precedence over the proper well-being and development of individuals in the agency.

Command-and-Control: Leaders in conventional fashion commonly undertake a directive technique, giving commands and waiting for compliance.

Self-Interest: Leaders would typically recognize private or organizational goals, sometimes at the expense of the broader community or employees' needs.

Transactional Nature: Relationships are transactional, based totally on an exchange of offerings for rewards or blessings.

SELFLESS LEADERSHIP

Inverted Pyramid of Leadership: Selfless leadership reverses the conventional pyramid, putting the leader at the bottom, helping, and serving the needs of their crew.

Emphasis on Empowerment: It prioritizes the boom, empowerment, and well-being of followers, fostering their non-public and professional development.

Collaborative Decision-Making: Leaders act as facilitators, encouraging participation and collaboration in choice-making tactics.

Others-Centric Approach: Leaders prioritize the wishes of their followers, seeking to serve and assist them selflessly.

Transformational Relationships: Focuses on building deep, significant relationships based on consideration, empathy, and mutual appreciation.

KEY CONTRASTS

Motivation: Traditional leaders may also encourage through rewards and punishment, while selfless leaders inspire through a shared vision and by way of serving as position fashions.

Goal orientation: Traditional fashions focus on attaining organizational goals, whereas selfless management emphasizes the growth and improvement of people to achieve collective targets.

Perception of Leadership: Traditional management regularly views leaders as authoritative figures, even as selfless management sees leaders as servants first, devoted to the increase in their fans.

Impact:

Employee Engagement: Selfless management tends to result in better worker delight, engagement, and commitment due to supportive and empowering surroundings.

ORGANIZATIONAL CULTURE: Selfless leadership fosters a culture of agreement, collaboration, and empathy, promoting an experience of belonging and shared purpose inside the company.

The assessment of conventional and selfless management fashions underscores the change in thinking from authoritative control to service-oriented management. Selfless leadership, with its attention to empathy, empowerment, and serving others, stands in comparison to conventional models that prioritize hierarchy, manipulation, and consequences. Understanding those variations is essential to appreciating the transformative ability of selfless leadership to nurture selfless leaders dedicated to the welfare of their groups.

PROS AND CONS OF SELFLESS LEADERSHIP

As with any leadership style, there are benefits and drawbacks to being a selfless leader. Before adopting selfless management as your management style, test some different pros and cons of being a selfless-first chief:

PROS

Fosters sturdy crew culture: Selfless leaders provide ownership to their crew individuals to boost their motivation, courage, and creativity.

Creates a human-focused way of life: Selfless leaders establish a human-centered lifestyle by means of fostering deep, trusting relationships with and among their teammates. This level of belief and connection allows groups to make selections in the best interest of the employer and everyone involved.

Boosts crew morale: A crew that feels seen and valued by their leader tends to have stronger integrity and display a better stage of pride in their work. Selfless leaders can enhance group morale across groups and assist in broadening future leaders by giving them opportunities to shine.

CONS

Formal authority can be misplaced. Because selfless leaders get down to one of these private levels with their teams, their formal authority is effortlessly misplaced. This can become hard when individuals take advantage of their chief's transparency. It can also be confusing when other leaders in the organization use an exclusive technique.

Time-intensive leadership style: selfless management necessitates a large amount of time, effort, and information. Selfless leaders ought to recognize their team participants to a professional and private degree so that they can help them to the fullest.

Team contributors may also need assistance with decision-making. By giving their group members opportunities to prove themselves, selfless leaders additionally risk overestimating and overburdening their teammates. Individuals who lack the essential bravery or self-assurance to make statistics-pushed choices independently may also revel in emotions of discouragement and confusion in their work surroundings, in which authority figures preserve huge power.

Have it in mind that the selfless leadership fashion may additionally want to align with your corporate overall performance control or incentive structures, which can often be centered on quick-time period dreams. However, you can nevertheless put in force the selfless leadership technique by maintaining authenticity, offering routes for your teammates, giving those opportunities to grow and expand their competencies, and constructing a strong network inside your group.

Chapter Ten

Characteristics of Successful and Unsuccessful Leadership

Good leadership is critical to any company, not only for growth and profitability but also for staff motivation and commitment. When 35% of people consider dealing with their superiors to be the most stressful part of their journey, it is time to find ways to improve.

What are the things to have to become good leaders? Are the characteristics of good leadership innate, or can they be learned? And what can you do to avoid hiring people with characteristics of what we call bad leadership?

What are the characteristics of leadership?

When it comes to leadership, there is some overlap between characteristics and abilities. A person's way of being (for example, whether he is charismatic or resilient) is usually innate, although people can enhance these characteristics over time. Instead, the way a person performs in his leadership role and his leadership characteristics (for example, knowing how to listen) are things that can be taught. Truly exceptional leadership has a combination of both and is always ready to improve in every possible way.

GOOD LEADERSHIP CHARACTERISTICS

In society in general and in companies in particular, the perception of what constitutes a set of characteristics of good leadership can vary. In the past, successful leadership was characterized by its determination and dogmatism. Today, leadership must be more empathetic, inclusive, and self-aware. However, a strategic and visionary mindset is a feature of leadership that always stays in style.

MOST IMPORTANT CHARACTERISTICS OF LEADERSHIP:

SELF-AWARENESS

Self-knowledge is essential for leadership to understand people's perceptions of it both inside and outside the organization. Leadership must also be aware of its limitations in terms of knowledge and skills and what aspects it should improve on.

As a leader, are you privy to your strengths and the regions in which you may continue to grow? Do you already know which verbal exchange techniques work great for you? Get into the habit of requesting remarks on an everlasting basis and be part of leadership training software as a part of your learning procedure. It may also be helpful to have a psychometric or personality test.

EMPATHY

Leadership empathy is an increasingly important feature. And now, after the pandemic, it is even more crucial. According to our research, 58% of employees in the UK would consider quitting their jobs if the company's leadership did not empathize with the needs of staff. Empathy is closely related to the well-being and mental health of staff. Based on our observations, it became apparent that 91% of the body of workers believed that the control needed to adopt a receptive approach toward their mental well-being. The task is that organizations generally tend to teach their leaders to be sturdy and infallible. There is a notion that talking about emotions somehow denotes weakness. However, the current landscape requires leadership to speak openly about emotions and show a compassionate attitude. A vital aspect needs to be addressed regularly and consistently, despite the absence of any commercial justification for doing so. Other essential skills of empathic leadership are knowing how to listen and being able to adapt the communication style to the needs of each group or person.

TRANSPARENCY

Like empathy, transparency is an increasingly important feature of leadership. It means dealing honestly and keeping the pledge word. For leadership, transparency is essential to instilling confidence in staff and strengthening relationships. According to our research, 62% of employees want transparency in social issues such as climate, diversity, and inclusion.

This may mean the need to put pressure on stakeholders so that all affected people can access relevant company statistics.

STRATEGIC THINKING

A mindset capable of looking at the big picture and visionary communication are key features that make great managers great leaders. Strategic leadership is comfortable thinking innovatively and creatively. He does not emphasize micromanaging; he is not afraid to leave the minute details in the hands of other valuable people on the team.

INTEGRITY

Integrity is more important than ever before, and there is a demand for a workforce made up of millennials and members of the generation. Honesty and accountability are key to building trust. Therefore, taking responsibility for mistakes and making mistakes is a fundamental feature of business leadership. And it is not only beneficial for human relationships; several studies show that companies with elevated levels of trust produce better financial results.

Once confidence is lost, it is not easy to regain it. However, incorporating this notion into opinion polls on staff commitment can help companies respond to any mistake in real time.

DETERMINATION

Leadership capable of making key decisions without consulting a committee is a valuable resource. The key is to show your team that, while you are a person willing to take risks, you are not exposed to unnecessary risks at random without weighing the consequences.

This feature of leadership was tested during the early days of the pandemic and during its advance. Many companies were forced to change course, something that was only immediately possible with determined leadership in command.

CHARISMA

This elusive feature is easy to identify but difficult to define. A memorable charism is one of the most notable features of countless renowned leaders, from Elon Musk to Jacinda Ardern. They express themselves with great clarity and have a remarkable power of persuasion, something that mobilizes those around them. There is a lot of debate about whether it is possible to learn the techniques that support charism, but without a doubt, it is something that cannot be faked.

INCLUSION

As agencies are searching to emerge as a more moral place, inclusion begins to dominate the floor. HBR and others mentioned the six traits of inclusive management, which permit embracing or even taking advantage of variations: knowledge, interest, bravery, cultural intelligence, commitment, and collaboration.

A good starting line is to recognize that in all management, there will constantly be internal biases and that, to perceive and get rid of them, awesome dedication is required.

RESILIENCE

The end times tested the resilience of leadership. Leadership must test its resilience regularly with minor challenges in order to prepare for future emergencies. This feature is related to mental health and well-being, and staff need to see that leadership prioritizes their care and expresses their discomfort when going through challenging times.

Characteristics of Poor Leadership

Are there really characteristics of bad leadership? There are certain characteristics that we must avoid when choosing leaders for a company.

UNETHICAL BEHAVIORS

In business, ethics is more important than ever, and leadership must exhibit ethical attitudes and behaviors. This includes getting involved, that is, acting on the matter when you hear or see unethical behaviors in other people rather than overlooking them.

ATTITUDE CLOSED

Curiosity and openness of mind are some of the most desired characteristics of leadership, so people who are closed to possibilities are unlikely to succeed as leaders.

ARROGANCE

Arrogant leadership is afraid to ask for advice and admit its mistakes or limitations. It is also characterized by not recognizing the deserved achievements of other people, which can be demoralizing. Self-confident leaders are pleased to hire talented people, as it does not see them as a threat.

EVASION OF CONFLICTS

A coveted feature of leadership is being able to quickly and fairly identify and deal with conflicts before they are exacerbated. While this demands some innate emotional intelligence, organizations can teach practical skills and provide advice and suggestions.

UNPREDICTABILITY

People feel unsafe when their leaders are unpredictable, which means that they do not always exhibit their best performance and have a lower predisposition to take risks.

Lack of vision

The ability to express the company's vision and reflect it in one's behavior is a key feature of leadership.

EGOCENTRISM

Self-centered leadership takes precedence over the rest and leaves staff and the organization second. Good leadership acts selflessly, a feature that only sometimes occurs naturally and takes a long time to develop.

INEFFECTIVE LEADERSHIP IN PERSPECTIVE

This positive leadership landscape is adequate, as effective leadership places value on organizations. Ineffective leaders are, fortunately, the exception and not the rule. Bad leadership is the following: Anyone who does not live in a cave is regularly exposed, even if only through the media, to people who exercise power negatively. A useful typology of ineffective leadership included titles such as incompetent, inflexible, excessive, cruel, corrupt, closed-minded, and malevolent. There are many ways to be an ineffective leader. While acknowledging that the cost of ineffective leadership is difficult to determine, they promoted the concept of not brushing off or embracing it, but alternatively acquiring further expertise about it if you want to fight it like every other disorder that causes harm, debilitation, and often even demise.

Chapter Eleven

Examinations of Leaders Demonstrating Selflessness

Here are case studies displaying selfless leaders who exemplify the principles of servant leadership:

MAHATMA GANDHI

Leadership Approach: Gandhi's management became rooted in selflessness, empathy, and service to others.

Selfless Leadership Traits: He led through instance, embracing humility and placing the desires of the marginalized at the leading edge of his motion.

Impact: His nonviolent approach to social change, centered on empowering the masses and promoting justice, inspired movements worldwide.

THE COMPASSIONATE LEADER

MOTHER TERESA

Leadership Approach: Mother Teresa epitomized selfless service and compassion in her work with the poorest of the terrible.

Selfless Leadership Traits: She committed her life to serving the needy and marginalized, offering care, compassion, and dignity.

Impact: Her unwavering commitment to the less fortunate hooked up a global legacy of humanitarian career.

HERB KELLEHER (SOUTHWEST AIRLINES)

Leadership Approach: Kelleher embraced a selfless leadership style, prioritizing employees' well-being.

Selfless Leadership Traits: He fostered a company tradition of valuing personnel, encouraging teamwork, and recognizing their contributions.

Impact: His approach contributed to Southwest Airlines' fulfillment, fostering supportive and tasty painting surroundings.

NELSON MANDELA

Leadership Approach: Mandela's leadership change was marked by forgiveness, reconciliation, and dedication to justice.

Selfless Leadership Traits: Despite adversity, he prioritized the desires of South Africa's diverse populace, selling solidarity and healing.

Impact: His altruistic guidance played a crucial role in the peaceful shift from apartheid to democracy in South Africa.

HOWARD SCHULTZ (STARBUCKS)

Leadership Approach: Schultz validated selfless management by prioritizing the well-being of Starbucks employees.

Selfless Leadership Traits: He implemented rules like healthcare blessings and stock alternatives for personnel, fostering a feeling of belonging and loyalty.

Impact: His people-centric method contributed to Starbucks' fulfillment and tremendous brand picture.

MALALA YOUSAFZAI

Leadership Approach: Malala exhibited selflessness in advocating for girls' training, no matter threats or adversity.

Selfless Leadership Traits: She courageously fought for schooling rights, amplifying the voices of marginalized ladies globally.

Impact: Her dedication led to an international reputation and catalyzed trade in training guidelines.

These case studies highlight leaders who exemplify selfless management by prioritizing others' wishes, demonstrating empathy, and fostering environments that empower and uplift people and groups. Their selfless movements and commitment to their careers serve as inspiring examples of leadership grounded in humility, compassion, and willpower to do the right thing.

THE INTERSECTION OF SELFLESSNESS AND SERVANT LEADERSHIP

The intersection of selflessness and servant leadership represents the convergence of two fundamental standards that profoundly affect the way leaders interact, encourage, and serve their followers.

Selfless management, at its core, revolves around the concept of leaders prioritizing the desires of others over their own. It involves a mindset in which leaders act as servants first, dedicating themselves to the growth, development, and well-being of their groups or communities. This approach emphasizes empathy, humility, and a real dedication to serving others.

Selflessness, in the context of management, embodies a similar ethos. It entails a willingness to set aside private pursuits, ego, and pursuits for the greater good of those being led. Selfless leaders' function comes from a standpoint in which their number one intention is to guide, uplift, and empower others, even supposing it is a method of non-public sacrifice.

The intersection among these two ideas is wherein management transcends mere authority and manipulation. It is a space where leaders harness the energy of empathy and humility to create environments of consideration, collaboration, and boom. Here, leaders do not search for recognition or glory; as an alternative, they derive fulfillment from the success and well-being of their teams or followers.

This intersection manifests as leaders who actively listen, empathize, and understand the wishes of their fans. They prioritize mentorship, assistance, and development, which are growing avenues for individuals to flourish. These leaders exhibit authenticity, showing integrity and transparency in their movements, fostering a tradition of consideration and appreciation.

Moreover, the intersection of selflessness and servant leadership encourages a shift in consciousness from individual achievements to collective achievements. It promotes an experience of shared purpose and a dedication to the more excellent, aligning the aspirations of both leaders and fans in the direction of a commonplace, imaginative, and prescient.

This intersection embodies a transformational method of leadership, one that goes beyond authority and management, emphasizing service, empathy, and an actual dedication to the well-being and growth of others. Leaders who navigate this intersection effectively create environments wherein people feel valued, inspired, and empowered, resulting in extra organizational achievement and societal effect.

DR. TYRONE SPEARS

Chapter Twelve

Developing Fostering Selfless Leadership through the Principles of Servant Leadership

Developing selfless leaders through the lens of servant leadership entails fostering an environment in which leaders prioritize the growth, well-being, and empowerment of their groups or followers over non-public targets or hierarchical authority. It is a transformative technique centered on serving others and cultivating a culture of empathy, collaboration, and consideration. This development system includes:

CULTIVATING A MINDSET OF SERVICE

Encouraging aspiring leaders to include an attitude that values careers for others as the cornerstone of leadership. This involves moving the focus from self-

hobby to information and assembling the wishes of their crew, fostering a sense of obligation toward the community they serve.

NURTURING EMPATHY AND EMOTIONAL INTELLIGENCE

Empathy is the middle ground of selfless leadership. Developing leaders who understand, are famous, and empathize with the reports, feelings, and traumatic conditions faced by their team participants foster deeper connections, ideals, and a supportive environment.

ENCOURAGING COLLABORATIVE DECISION-MAKING

Selfless leaders involve their team members in selection-making procedures. This collaborative approach now not only values various views but also instills a feeling of possession and commitment amongst group contributors toward shared desires.

PRIORITIZING PERSONAL AND PROFESSIONAL GROWTH

Creating possibilities for continuous study, improvement, and mentorship is essential to nurturing selfless leaders. This includes investing in their private growth, encouraging them to increase their abilities, and presenting mentorship to enhance their management skills.

MODELING SELFLESS LEADERSHIP BEHAVIOR

Effective leaders lead by example. They exhibit selfless leadership developments by actively serving their group individuals, showing humility, and displaying a real commitment to their growth and achievement.

PROMOTING A CULTURE OF ACCOUNTABILITY AND SUPPORT

Building a lifestyle where duty is balanced with aid and encouragement is critical. Leaders' ought to encourage chance-taking, gaining knowledge from failures, and supplying a safety net that fosters growth in place of punishment.

REINFORCING THE VISION OF COLLECTIVE SUCCESS

Selfless leaders inspire and motivate by emphasizing the collective achievement of the team or organization over individual achievements. They talk about a compelling vision that aligns everybody toward a shared motive.

Recognizing and Celebrating Contributions:

Recognizing and valuing the efforts made by members of a team is crucial. Recognizing their efforts cultivates an experience of belonging and encourages a culture wherein each person's contributions are valued.

Developing selfless leaders through servant management entails a holistic method that prioritizes serving others, fostering empathy, nurturing growth, and creating a lifestyle that encourages collaboration, duty, and a shared imagination and prescience. It is about creating surroundings in which leaders lead with a focus on empowering and supporting others, and in the end, using organizational achievement via the collective efforts of a committed and stimulated crew.

LEADERSHIP CHARACTER: THE ESSENCE OF LEADING

Leadership character is made up of values, traits, and the readability of motives that determine what one desires to be as a leader. This is expressed in consistency of behavior, the degree to which a leader's actions agree with his words. Most people have experienced, either in their work or in their personal lives, a leader who served as a model of leadership character. It was that leader who showed a true interest in you as a person, who was his mentor or who supported him while growing professionally, and who always made decisions based on deep clarity of purpose and intention. It is this type of leader that attracts people and inspires them to give their maximum energy.

We have observed that only a few businesses (or leaders) outline the crucial elements of the leadership character in this identical way. Our studies have diagnosed more than sixteen male or female character factors that have been linked to management fulfillment. Wilson Learning has categorized them into these three essential additives: personal character, social character, and organizational character.

Personal Character. The character of remaining firm and determined in the face of adversity.

Social Character. Show respect, be compassionate, and value individual differences.

Organizational Character. The will to put the needs of the organization and its clients ahead of personal needs.

Effective leaders demonstrate a balance of these three components as core values.

The leadership character is the inspiration or essence of all-powerful leadership. It is likewise one of the least tangible components of leadership. Some recollect that the leadership character cannot be evolved by people who have or do not have it. We consider that now, not only can humans broaden their management character, but they must achieve this if they aspire to enhance their overall performance as leaders. In other words, the leader cannot advance without growing in character. We also recognize that organizations no longer develop leadership personnel in the same way that they expand other management abilities. Developing leadership character requires getting leaders to recognize their value structures, boost self-consciousness, enjoy the effect of character on their lives, and spoil old thought styles. Through a mixture of reviews, education, and help, you will create the vital reflection needed to increase leadership character.

ROLES: THE LITERACY WAY

Wilson Learning's comprehensive leadership model

While leadership character is the basis of effective leadership, it is not in and of itself sufficient. Unless this foundation is complemented by the skills and knowledge necessary to act based on those values and principles, the leader will not be able to produce the tangible results necessary for the creation of organizational success.

Our angle, based on each in-depth study and realistic reveal, is that the abilities important to execute effective leadership can be described as four primary roles that each must satisfy: visionary, tactical, facilitator, and contributor.

These roles complement each other, bringing their strengths to effective leadership. For instance, the visionary makes a specialty of placing courses, while the tactical ensures that sports occur to gain imagination and prescience. The facilitator guarantees that each group of individuals and stakeholders is nicely involved, even as the contributor ensures that the chief's abilities are being carried out. These four roles outline the contradictory duties of a leader—often the best mission of management. Being a notable chief means being able to successfully stabilize those four capabilities and efficiently integrate them into the leadership character.

Different situations require diverse types of leadership. Therefore, the importance of each function varies by level and by organization. However, all four roles are essential for effective leadership at all levels. A front-line supervisor may need to put more emphasis on the tactical role but must recognize the visionary role. A senior executive ought to place greater emphasis on the visionary position and less on the taxpayer, leaving maximum implementation problems to the executive crew. However, it is going to remain vital—and frequently essential—that choices are made that require a CEO to use his competencies as a taxpayer. Effective leaders lead with the attitude of all four roles.

The Visionary.

The visionary guides personal and organizational growth with the aid of inspiring, imaginative, and prescient ideas. While vital at all levels of the agency, the role of the visionary takes unique bureaucracy as the leader's scope of management expands. Management needs to have deep information on their competitive surroundings and then use those records to create a vision and method for the business enterprise. It is also critical to include others in refining that vision and the percentage of that vision in a way that promotes commitment to obtain it. However, even the front-line supervisors (at a minimum) ought to translate the business enterprise's vision and method into jobs that provide experience for their employees and apprehend the needs of their inner clients.

The Tactical.

If the visionary asks, "What?" the tactical asks, "How?". In the tactical function, the leader ensures that business consequences are accomplished through effective control of tasks and responsibilities. For the tactical to be effective, you must plan work activities that are achievable and challenging for the employee; you must properly delegate tasks, objectives, and decisions to others; monitor and monitor implementation to ensure that the organization's objectives are met; and support others in their performance.

THE FACILITATOR.

The facilitator creates an environment of collaboration and teamwork to ensure effective working relationships—a key duty of the lowest tiers of management. In the position of facilitator, powerful leaders manipulate struggle, build groups, and observe communication talents to generate actions and selections. By fulfilling his role as facilitator, the chief creates surroundings wherein everybody feels valued and knows what his contribution is to the achievement of the organization.

THE CONTRIBUTOR.

The Contributor. Finally, the contributor focuses on creating the organization's success using personal talents. Although leaders are not the ones doing the homework, they are often called to use their creativity, problem-solving skills, and decision-making abilities. Senior managers must understand what decision-making really is like in the organization.

INTEGRATED LEADERSHIP: PERSONAL PERFORMANCE AND REALIZATION

By integrating the four roles—the visionary, the tactical, the facilitator, and the contributor—with the fundamental basis of the leadership character, the necessary conditions are created to achieve performance with personal fulfillment. We believe that both performance and personal fulfillment are essential to maintaining high performance—that people will only be able to maintain high performance if they feel fulfilled, and that people will only feel fulfilled at work if they have elevated levels of performance.

Integrated leadership creates the necessary conditions for performance and personal fulfillment. The inability of a leader to assume any of the four roles reduces the feeling of personal fulfillment, performance, or both. Without vision, employees do not get the fulfillment they feel knowing that they are contributing to a greater good. With tactical knowledge, employees find it easier to determine whether their actions are contributing to the success of the organization. Without facilitation management, the work environment can be hostile and unproductive. Employees need a significant sense of contribution from leaders to perform performance models. In the absence of a leadership character, employees feel the need to reflect on the values of their leaders. They will adjust their level of commitment to the success of the organization according to this feeling.

Chapter Thirteen

Profiles of Leadership

All leaders, regardless of their level, must fulfill all four roles. But they do not need to do it with the same emphasis or depth all the time. The emphasis on each role should vary, depending on the specific responsibilities of each leader. The significance of each leadership function in the picture illustration of the version illustrates how unique leadership positions require extraordinary profiles to be powerful. Although there are countless profiles, we define below the three that are most commonplace.

Leadership for Performance the Leadership for Performance profile is typical for a front line of supervisors or managers (e.g., sales managers, supervisors, chief accountants). However, in some organizations, performance leadership is the fundamental profile for department managers or even division directors.

Performance leadership requires strong taxpayer and tactical leadership skills to be responsible for the tasks and goals you have. Performance leadership is focused on ensuring that all employees add value and are often expected to have answers to specific technical or functional questions. While these managers need to translate the organization's strategies into day-to-day workgroup objectives effectively and occasionally must direct the team's efforts, most of their time is devoted to the tactical aspects of "making the job done."

Leadership for Growth the Leadership for Growth profile is the most balanced of the three types, representing a typical mid-level profile or division manager in a medium to large organization.

Growth Leaders require skills that go from moderate to strong in all four leadership roles. Leaders for Growth are expected to execute the strategy, even if they have yet to participate in its definition. They often must work with and influence their peers, even if they have no authority over them, and deal with interpersonal conflicts within the organization. Leaders for Growth also need strong tactical skills as they manage other leaders to achieve their goals. They are often called to contribute their unique talents to solve specific functional problems or make critical decisions. Without a doubt, the leader with the Leadership for Growth profile wears many hats.

STRATEGIC LEADERSHIP. The strategic leadership profile is that of a high-level leader (e.g., Division Vice President and superiors). The most important roles of the strategic leader are the visionary and the facilitator, as those leaders are anticipated to power trade, create an imaginative and prescient vision for the future of the organization, and broaden techniques to achieve the imaginative and prescient vision. To achieve this, strategic leaders need strong facilitation skills to obtain various functions and groups of employees who work together towards a shared positive future.

The competencies inherent in this profile are often limited to supporting the tactical leadership efforts of functional directors. At the same time, the skills of the contributing role are normally reserved for more critical situations. High-level executive leaders who spend a lot of time on tactical and tax-paying roles are not considered effective in executive functions because they clearly need to develop their direct subordinates sufficiently.

INTEGRATION OF ESSENCE AND WAY

We believe that, like the four management roles, the leadership character ought to be emphasized irrespective of where or at what stage a pacesetter works. The leadership character may be expressed in any other way, depending on the position of the leader, the values of the enterprise, or even the unique business that it faces. Still, it is not true that character is extra essential as it moves in the direction of higher stages of leadership. This is because people need a frontrunner who has a solid foundation in what he is as a frontrunner, specifically in times of change. With so many factors disrupting the painting's surroundings today, leaders with a well-developed experience of themselves can provide a beacon of balance: consistency between desires and values that employees need to stay targeted at the assignment, no matter their stage inside the organization.

dr. tyrone spears

Chapter Fourteen

Closing Thoughts on The Selfless Leader

The concept of a selfless leader, through the concepts of servant leadership, becomes obtrusive in that effective leadership transcends mere authority and instructions. It embraces a profound ethos of service, empathy, and commitment to others' boom and well-being.

The expertise of selfless leadership via the lens of servant leadership concepts is well-known as a change of thinking in management paradigms. It highlights the transformative energy of leaders who prioritize the wishes of their fans, fostering environments built on acceptance as true, collaboration, and shared reason.

In its middle, the idea of a selfless chief embodies humility, empathy, and a constant dedication to serving others. It underscores the significance of leaders who lead by means of, for instance, placing the pastimes of their crew members or followers above their own.

The principles of selfless management offer a roadmap for cultivating selfless leaders who inspire, empower, and increase the ones around them. These leaders create environments in which human beings feel valued, supported, and encouraged to achieve their full potential.

The essence of selfless leadership lies in its potential to create a ripple effect of advantageous alternatives, both within groups and in a broader society. It fosters a culture of compassion, inclusivity, and collective growth, paving the way for a more empathetic and impactful approach to management.

As it navigates the complexities of management in an ever-evolving international context, embracing the principles of selfless management to nurture selfless leaders emerges as an effective catalyst for fostering more healthy, sustainable, and motive-driven groups and communities. It is a call to action for leaders to embody career, empathy, and a commitment to the extra mile, fostering a legacy of management that leaves a lasting and fine impact on the arena. By prioritizing compassion, inclusivity, and collective growth, leaders can create a work environment that values the well-being and development of their team members. This approach not only leads to increased productivity and success, but also cultivates a sense of fulfillment and purpose among employees. Ultimately, embracing selfless management principles can transform organizations into thriving communities where individuals are motivated to contribute their best and make a positive impact on the world. Selfless management principles encourage leaders to lead by example and foster a culture of trust and respect. By empowering their team members and providing them with the necessary resources and support, leaders can unleash their full potential and inspire them to achieve greatness. Additionally, embracing selfless leadership can also help organizations attract top talent and retain employees, as individuals are more likely to stay in a work environment that values their well-being and offers opportunities for growth.

Made in the USA
Las Vegas, NV
05 July 2024

91868763R00049